The Poetry Show 1

David Orme and James Sale
Directors of the Schools' Poetry Association

MACMILLAN
EDUCATION

First published 1987

Published by
MACMILLAN EDUCATION LTD
Houndmills, Basingstoke, Hampshire RG21 2XS
and London
Companies and representatives
throughout the world

Designed by Linda Reed

Illustrated by David Eyre

Printed in Hong Kong

British Library Cataloguing in Publication Data
Orme, David
The poetry show.
1
1. Poetics
I. Title   II. Sale, James
808.1   PN1042
ISBN 0-333-39785-1

Contents

Acknowledgements

The editors and publishers wish to thank the following who have kindly given permission for the use of copyright material:

Faber and Faber Publishers for 'The Combat', from *The Collected Poems of Edwin Muir*;

The National Trust for Places of Historic Interest and Natural Beauty and Macmillan London Ltd for 'The Way Through the Woods' by Rudyard Kipling, from *The Definitive Edition of Rudyard Kipling's Verse*;

Pisces Press for 'Making Poetry', © Anne Stevenson 1985;

The Literary Trustees of Walter de la Mare and The Society of Authors as their Representative for 'The Listeners' by Walter de la Mare;

Granada Publishing Limited for 'in Just' taken from *The Complete Poems 1913–1962* by e.e. cummings;

Nick Toczek for 'Prose Poem';

Geoffrey Holloway and Patricia Pogson for 'Trafalgar Square' (1) and (6), 'Indian Haiku', 'Snowflake', 'Haiku';

The Reader's Digest Association Ltd for the shape words on pages 19 and 21, © 1967 and 1977;

Editions Gallimard for 'Calligram (15 May 1915) and Coeur (Heart)', from *Calligrammes* by Guillaume Apollinaire, © Editions Gallimard 1925;

Faber and Faber Publishers for 'Days' from *The Whitsun Weddings* by Philip Larkin;

A D Peters and Company Ltd for 'There's Something Sad', from *The Mersey Sound* by Roger McGough;

Adolfini Collection Trust, Bristol and John Furnival for a detail from 'Manhattan';

Andre Deutsch for 'The Firefly' and 'The Rhinoceros', from *I Wouldn't have Missed it* by Ogden Nash;

Wes Magee for 'A–Z of Headlines', 'A New Year', 'Robin', 'Legend', 'North York Moors: November', 'Breakdown', 'Electric Household', 'Visitor', 'Cries of London', 'A Marked Man';

Mango Chutney for 'A-Stack' and 'Suckerslick';

Barry Heath for 'First Day at School';

Cambridge University Press for 'Insec' Lesson' by Valerie Bloom, from *I Like that Stuff* edited by Morag Styles;

Brian Hinton for four lines from 'Yes, in 10 days you can become a poet';

William Heinemann Ltd for 'The Sea', from *The Wandering Moon* by James Reeves;

Faber and Faber Publishers for six lines from 'Tattoo', from *The Collected Poems of Wallace Stevens*;

Angus and Robertson (UK) Ltd for 'The Beach' by William Hart-Smith, from *Selected Poems 1936–1984* by William Hart-Smith;

Faber and Faber Publishers for 'In a Station of the Metro', from *Collected Shorter Poems* by Ezra Pound;

Black Sparrow Press for 'This Smoky Winter Morning' and 'About an Excavation' by Charles Reznikoff;

Secker and Warburg Ltd for 'A Windy Day' by Andrew Young, from *The Poetical Works of Andrew Young*;

The Hogarth Press for 'Fetching Cows', from *Measures* by Norman McCaig;

Judith Nicholls for 'Celtic Burial Stones'.

The authors and publishers wish to acknowledge the following photographic sources: the Trustees of the National Portrait Gallery, London, p. 38; Peter and Ginny Barnfield, p. 80; Yer Own Stuff, p. 47.

Every effort has been made to trace all the copyright holders, but if any have been inadvertently overlooked the publishers will be pleased to make the necessary arrangements at the first opportunity.

Preface

Lewis Carroll writes:

> For first you write a sentence,
> And then you chop it small;
> Then mix the bits, and sort them out
> Just as they chance to fall:
> The order of the phrases makes
> No difference at all.

The Poetry Show is an attempt to show pupils and teachers just how poetry is written. For poetry is not a result of chance, but of skilful craftsmanship, and the order of phrases makes every difference in the world.

Simply used as an anthology, *The Poetry Show* provides ample and varied poetry material. The familiar and less well-known, modern and past, accessible and more challenging sorts of poetry crowd these pages. However, *The Poetry Show* is far more than an anthology: it is a systematic effort to explain poetry, to demonstrate poetry's techniques, to raise questions for class discussion, to point the directions towards profitable class and individual work. There is here abundant material to read, to discuss, to work with.

The Poetry Show series follows a common pattern: six chapters – Introduction, Rhythm/Form, Rhyme/Sound, Words, Imagery, Drafting/ The Living Poet. This is to concentrate attention on the specific features of poetry. Within these chapters the pattern tends to be three or four short units where narrative text is interspersed with

■ Discussion material
  and
□ Work suggestions

Ideas are introduced sequentially, but these books are ideal for dipping into: even the non-specialist teacher could confidently teach a lesson, say by turning to 'Cinquain', and any pupil could understand the form through the clear, diagrammatic explanation and lively illustrations.

A special feature is the emphasis on living poets: these are introduced in the last chapter where their techniques of writing are fully examined.

In addition to the copious work suggestions within each chapter, the first five chapters are followed by 'Endpieces' – to involve the whole class in a range of varied and interesting poetry activities.

In short these books help teachers cover every aspect of poetry suitable for pupils from Middle School to GCSE level, providing a visually and intellectually stimulating challenge to pupils.

Some will doubtless argue that we 'murder to dissect' and that in analysing the techniques of poetry we are spoiling the poem. The confusion here is largely one of terminology. We do not advocate 'taking a poem to bits' or treating poetry as an object for comprehension exercises. On the contrary, we believe that a full appreciation of poetry comes from looking at it closely. The alternative is casual acquaintance, and how can this be said to heighten the experience of reading and writing poetry?

As Directors of the Schools' Poetry Association we have been increasingly confronted by teachers requesting more information on the technical aspects of writing, and how to present this kind of material to students. We believe that *The Poetry Show* goes a long way towards meeting such requests. We also believe that the move towards writing as a craft-based activity is the way forward for poetry teaching in schools.

David Orme
James Sale

Wonder's Mystery Sound

1 Poetry's Peacock: Wonder

I saw a Peacock with a fiery tail

I saw a Peacock with a fiery tail,
I saw a blazing Comet drop down hail,
I saw a Cloud with ivy circled round,
I saw a sturdy Oak creep on the ground,
I saw a Pismire swallow up a whale,
I saw a raging Sea brim full of ale,
I saw a Venice Glass sixteen foot deep,
I saw a Well full of men's tears that weep,
I saw their Eyes all in a flame of fire,
I saw a House as big as the moon and higher,
I saw the Sun even in the midst of night,
I saw the Man that saw this wondrous sight.

ANON

What extraordinary sights! Poetry helps us to notice or imagine all the wonder of the world. But are all these sights *possible*?

■   I saw a Pismire swallow up a whale
(A 'pismire' is an ant!) Can this be? Can there really be
        a Cloud with ivy circled round
or would
        a sturdy Oak creep on the ground?

☐ Draw a picture for one of the lines. Then write a poem with every line beginning 'I saw . . .' Make your sights as extraordinary as you can.

Poetry manages to contain both wonder *and* sense. But sometimes its sense is hidden! Let's look at the poem again:

    I saw a Peacock
    with a <u>fiery tail</u>, I saw a bla<u>z</u>ing Comet
    drop down <u>hail</u>, I saw a Cloud
    with <u>ivy</u> circled round, . . .

■ Does it make more sense now? How? Why was it written out in the first way?

☐ You complete the poem. Write it out with different line breaks, so that it makes more ordinary sense.

☐ Repeating 'I saw' in each line makes the poem easy to remember. Try to learn it by heart.

2 Poetry's Creature: Mystery

Poetry, we say, combines wonder and sense. It also deals with mystery. When we have mystery, we have questions. When we have questions, we want answers. Read *The Combat*.

☐ Make a list of all the questions about the poem you want answered. We can think of at least six.

The Combat

It was not meant for human eyes,
That combat on the shabby patch
Of clods and trampled turf that lies
Somewhere beneath the sodden skies
For eye of toad or adder to catch.

And having seen it I accuse
The crested animal in his pride,
Arrayed in all the royal hues
Which hide the claws he well can use
To tear the heart out of the side.

Body of leopard, eagle's head
And whetted beak, and lion's mane,
And frost-grey hedge of feathers spread
Behind — he seemed of all things bred.
I shall not see his like again.

As for his enemy, there came in
A soft round beast as brown as clay;
All rent and patched his wretched skin;
A battered bag he might have been,
Some old used thing to throw away.

4   Yet he awaited face to face
The furious beast and the swift attack.
Soon over and done. That was no place
Or time for chivalry or for grace.
The fury had him on his back.

And two small paws like hands flew out
To right and left as the trees stood by.
One would have said beyond a doubt
This was the very end of the bout,
But that the creature would not die.

For ere the death-stroke he was gone,
Writhed, whirled, huddled into his den,
Safe somehow there. The fight was done,
And he had lost who had all but won.
But oh his deadly fury then.

A while the place lay blank, forlorn,
Drowsing as in relief from pain.
The cricket chirped, the grating thorn
Stirred, and a little sound was born.
The champions took their posts again.

And all began. The stealthy paw
Slashed out and in. Could nothing save
These rags and tatters from the claw?
Nothing. And yet I never saw
A beast so helpless and so brave.

And now, while the trees stand watching, still
The unequal battle rages there.
The killing beast that cannot kill
Swells and swells in his fury till
You'd almost think it was despair.

EDWIN MUIR

■ The sort of questions that occur to us are:
  – Why 'not meant for human eyes'?
  – Where and when did this happen?
  – What sort of animals are these?
  – Why could the creature not die?
  – And why could the other creature not win?
  – Why were they fighting?

☐ Choose either the five lines beginning

> Body of leopard . . .

or

> As for his enemy . . .

Write them out and illustrate them. Invent names for the two animals.

Perhaps not knowing all the answers helps our imaginations work. We cannot say precisely what the poem means – it means many things.

■ It is about two creatures fighting. Is it also about victims and attackers? Good and evil? What do you think?
☐ Make up two imaginary animals and a relationship between them – love, hate, fear, resentment . . . . Write a poem describing the animals, and set down what happens between them. You need not give your two animals names.

3 Poetry's Way: Sound

I saw a Peacock is fun to read. *The Combat* is exciting, and perhaps we feel pity for the 'brave' and 'helpless' beast.

Poetry moves our feelings. This is important. It helps even more to hear a poem read aloud: it helps our understanding; it lets us hear the sound of the poem; it emphasises important words and phrases.

☐ Read *The Way through the Woods* to yourself, then listen to it read aloud. Finally, read it aloud yourself, slowly.

The Way through the Woods

They shut the road through the woods
Seventy years ago.
Weather and rain have undone it again,
And now you would never know
There was once a road through the woods
Before they planted the trees.

It is underneath the coppice and heath,
And the thin anemones.
Only the keeper sees
That, where the ring dove broods,
And the badgers roll at ease,
There was once a road through the woods.

Yet, if you enter the woods
Of a summer evening late,
When the night-air cools on the trout-ringed pools
Where the otter whistles his mate,
(They fear not men in the woods,
Because they see so few)
You will hear the beat of a horse's feet
And the swish of a skirt in the dew,
Steadily cantering through
The misty solitudes,
As though they perfectly knew
The old lost road through the woods . . .
But there is no road through the woods.

RUDYARD KIPLING

■ What words and phrases did you find repeated? Why do you think the poet keeps mentioning them?

□ Now try arranging a choral reading of the poem. One possible arrangement might be:

> Girls: 'They shut the road . . .
> . . . they planted the trees.'
> Boys: 'It is underneath . . .
> . . . road through the woods.'
> All: 'Yet, if you enter . . .
> . . . The old lost road through the woods . . .'

One girl and one boy: 'But there is no road through the woods.'

Try different group sizes for different parts of the poem.

■ Which group sizes work best? Why? Pay attention to individual lines: compare reading 'And the swish of a skirt in the dew' with 'Steadily cantering through'. What do you notice? Think about the 'speed' of the line.

The Way through the Woods is, like *The Combat,* mysterious.

□ What questions do you want answered about the poem? Make a list. Invent your own answers to your questions. Use these answers to write a short story about *The Way through the Woods*.

□ Read the poem *The Listeners* in the anthology at the end of this chapter. Imagine you are the traveller. Write a poem describing the adventures of your 'Journey through the Woods'. Perhaps you meet 'the keeper'. What happens?

ANTHOLOGY 1

Ring-a-ring-o'-roses,
Pocketful of posies,
Hiroshima
We all fall down!

ANON

Out of his hole to steal he stole,
His bag of chink he chunk,
And many a wicked smile he smole,
And many a wink he wunk.

ANON

Making Poetry

You have to inhabit poetry
if you want to make it.

And what's *to inhabit?*

To be in the habit of, to wear
words, sitting in the plainest worldlight –
in the silk of morning, in the shoe of night;
a feeling, bare and frondish in surprising air;
familiar, rare.

And what's *to make?*

To be and to become words' passing
weather; to serve the girl on terrible
terms, embark on voyages over voices,
evade the ego-hill, the misery-well,
the siren hiss of *publish, success, publish, success,*
success, success.

And why inhabit, make, inherit poetry?

Oh, it's the shared comedy of the worst
blessed; the sound leading the hand;
a wordlife running from mind to mind
through the washed rooms of the simple senses;
one of those haunted, undefendable,
    unpoetic crosses
we have to find.

ANNE STEVENSON

The Listeners

'Is there anybody there?' said the Traveller,
   Knocking on the moonlit door;
And his horse in the silence champed the grasses
   Of the forest's ferny floor:
And a bird flew up out of the turret,
   Above the Traveller's head:
And he smote upon the door again a second time;

'Is there anybody there?' he said.
But no one descended to the Traveller;
    No head from the leaf-fringed sill
Leaned over and looked into his grey eyes,
    Where he stood perplexed and still.
But only a host of phantom listeners
    That dwelt in the lone house then
Stood listening in the quiet of the moonlight
    To that voice from the world of men:
Stood thronging the faint moonbeams on the dark stair,
    That goes down to the empty hall,
Hearkening in an air stirred and shaken
    By the lonely Traveller's call.
And he felt in his heart their strangeness,
    Their stillness answering his cry,
While his horse moved, cropping the dark turf,
    'Neath the starred and leafy sky;
For he suddenly smote on the door, even
    Louder, and lifted his head: —
'Tell them I came, and no one answered,
    That I kept my word,' he said.
Never the least stir made the listeners,
    Though every word he spake
Fell echoing through the shadowiness of the still house
    From the one man left awake:
Ay, they heard his foot upon the stirrup,
    And the sound of iron on stone,
And how the silence surged softly backward,
    When the plunging hoofs were gone.

WALTER DE LA MARE

The Green Eye of the Little Yellow God

There's a one-eyed yellow idol to the north of Khatmandu,
There's a little marble cross below the town;
And a broken-hearted woman tends the grave of 'Mad' Carew,
While the Yellow God forever gazes down.

He was known as 'Mad' Carew by the subs at Khatmandu,
He was better than they felt inclined to tell;
But, for all his foolish pranks, he was worshipped in the ranks,
And the Colonel's daughter smiled on him as well.

He had loved her all along, with the passion of the strong,
And that she returned his love was plain to all.
She was nearly twenty-one, and arrangements were begun
To celebrate her birthday with a ball.

He wrote to ask what present she would like from 'Mad' Carew:
They met next day as he dismissed a squad;
And jestingly she made pretence that nothing else would do
But the green eye of the Little Yellow God.

On the night before the dance 'Mad' Carew seemed in a trance,
And they chaffed him as they puffed at their cigars;
But for once he failed to smile, and he sat alone awhile,
Then went out into the night beneath the stars.

He returned before the dawn, with his shirt and tunic torn,
And a gash across his temples dripping red;
He was patched up right away, and he slept all through the day,
And the Colonel's daughter watched beside his bed.

He woke at last and asked her if she'd send his tunic through.
She brought it, and he thanked her with a nod.
He bade her search the pocket, saying, 'That's from "Mad" Carew,'
And she found *the little green eye of the god*.

She upbraided poor Carew in the way that women do,
Though both her eyes were strangely hot and wet;
But she wouldn't take the stone, and Carew was left alone
With the jewel that he'd chanced his life to get.

When the ball was at its height, on that still and tropic night,
She thought of him, and hastened to his room;
As she crossed the barrack square she could hear the dreamy air
Of a waltz tune softly stealing thro' the gloom.

His door was open wide, with silver moonlight shining through,
The place was wet and slippy where she trod;
An ugly knife lay buried in the heart of 'Mad' Carew,
'Twas the vengeance of the Little Yellow God.

There's a one-eyed yellow idol to the north of Khatmandu,
There's a little marble cross below the town;
And a broken-hearted woman tends the grave of 'Mad' Carew,
While the Yellow God forever gazes down.

J. MILTON HAYES

ENDPIECE: Performing Poetry

A project for small groups or the whole class. Select from the poetry you have written, and the poems in Anthology 1. You are going to produce a poetry show for a live audience (assembly) or a cassette tape (say, for another class).

Choosing the material Aim at a mixture of humorous, serious/long, short/personal poems. Decide: what is the best order? How long should the show be?

Readers Who is going to read a poem? Do some poems require more than one reader? Are you going to introduce the poems in any way? Remember that there will be a difference between speaking for a live audience and speaking into a microphone. If you are speaking to a live audience, will you learn the poem by heart?

Review Write a review of the performance (not your own!).

Shape Up

1 Line Up

> I always eat peas with honey, I've done it all my life, they do taste
> kind of funny, but it keeps them on the knife.

■ *Poetry* is a very different kind of writing from prose. Which do you
think the first paragraph is? How can you tell?

□ Write the paragraph out as a poem. (The poem is included in the
collection at the end of this chapter.) Sometimes the difference
between prose and poetry is hard to spot, but usually you can start
from the fact that poetry *looks* different. Now read this:

> What are days for? Days are where we live. They come, they
> wake us time and time over. They are to be happy in: Where
> can we live but days? Ah, solving that question brings the priest
> and the doctor in their long coats running over the fields.

□ This has been printed here as prose, but it was written as a poem –
Days, by Philip Larkin. Write it out with the breaks of a poem.

■ Compare your version with Philip Larkin's poem at the end of this
chapter. Discuss the differences between your version and his: was
it difficult to decide where to break the lines? Did you then have to
change anything else?

□ Write a short paragraph explaining why you ended the lines where
you did.

The *line* 'measures' poetry: the longer the line, the more you can say.
Capital letters show a new line is beginning – but not always!

in Just-
spring when the world is mud-
luscious the little
lame balloonman

whistles   far   and wee

and eddieandbill come
running from marbles and
piracies and it's
spring

when the world is puddle-wonderful

the queer
old balloonman whistles
far   and   wee
and bettyandisbel come dancing

from hop-scotch and jump-rope and

it's
spring
and
      the

            goat-footed

balloonMan   whistles
far
and
wee

e.e. cummings

☐ Only two words have capitals. Which ones? And four would
   normally have capitals, but not here. Which ones?

■ Discuss these words. Look closely at the language:

              little   queer   goat-footed
    lame balloonman   old balloonman   balloonMan.

Which of these three descriptions is the odd one out? Why? Does
'goat-footed' give us a clue to the identity of the balloonMan? And
does his identity explain why there might be a capital M?

☐ Find out all you can about Pan. Use this information to write a poem called *Pan*.

■ The poem is about spring. What suggestions of spring are there? The poet has made up some words: 'mud-luscious' and 'puddle-wonderful'. What could these words mean?

Turn to page 42 for more about new words.

2 Form: Haiku

Prose Poem

I am a prose poem.
This is my second line
and this my third.
I consist of fifteen lines in all,
these made up from a total
of seventy-one words.
I am neither beautiful
nor am I ugly,
and I differ from all other poems
in that I describe nothing
except myself.
Where, when and by whom I was written
is therefore unimportant.
I have no title, and finish
abruptly.

NICK TOCZEK

Poetry? Prose? We said that sometimes it's difficult to decide! What do you think this *Prose Poem* is? Is Nick Toczek right? Are there fifteen   . lines? Seventy-one words? Check. If there are, the poet has done some careful planning before he wrote.

More useful than counting words is counting syllables in a line.

Doctor Bell fell down the well
And broke his collar-bone.
Doctors should attend the sick
And leave the well alone.

ANON

□ Count the syllables in each line of this poem. What is the pattern? These syllable counts often help give poetry its shape.

□ Choose a paragraph in this book, and write it out in lines of four syllables:

> Poetry? Prose?
> We said that some-
> times it's diffi-
> cult to decide.
> Is Nick Toczek
> right? . . .

■ Is this a 'prose poem'? Will any syllables do? Compare it with Nick Toczek's *Prose Poem*. Are his words more carefully chosen?

Haiku (pronounced 'high-koo') came from Japan. They are poems of three lines:

Trafalgar Square (1)

Line 1 has five syllables
Line 2 has seven syllables
Line 3 has five syllables

The fountains' can-can:
ostrich plumy – glittering
flesh tints, champagne skirts.

GEOFFREY HOLLOWAY

Here's a picture that illustrates the poem.

■ What do the fountain in Trafalgar Square and the frilly skirts of the can-can dancers have in common in the poem? In the picture?

■ The skirt is described as 'champagne'. Does this give a clue to the kind of revelry linked in the poet's mind?

Geoffrey Holloway works like a painter, doesn't he? Asked to sketch something with only three strokes of his paintbrush, he succeeds! He gets the shape of the fountain, and the spirit of the place as well, in his three lines.

This next haiku shows another view of Trafalgar Square:

Trafalgar Square (6)

Again the pigeons.
One on that boy's head. Behold:
Big Chief Sitting Bird!

□ Draw a picture to show Geoffrey Holloway's humorous view.

■ Discuss what else you might associate with Trafalgar Square, or a similar place.

□ Write haiku to describe your view of such a scene.

When you are used to writing haiku, you can sometimes break the 5–7–5 pattern. Sometimes what you want to say will be even more effective if you bend the pattern. Always say what you mean, as Patricia Pogson does:

Indian Haiku (1)

At noon no water,
At dusk no electricity.
This is India.

PATRICIA POGSON

■ How is this not 'exactly' right? Try to make the poem fit the 5–7–5 pattern. What happens? Is any word replaceable in this poem?

□ Form into groups of three. Choose a place you all know personally. Discuss it – features, colours, and ideas. Then, each contribute one line of the haiku.

□ Write a second haiku, but this time agree all of the lines between you, checking the number of syllables. Was that an easier way of working?

□ Read your two haiku out to the other groups.

3 Form: Cinquain

Cinquains were invented by the American poet, Adelaide Crapsey:

Triad

These be
Three silent things:
The falling snow . . . the hour
Before the dawn . . . the mouth of one
Just dead.

ADELAIDE CRAPSEY

☐ Check the number of lines, the syllable count for each line.

Haiku have 17 syllables in total. Cinquains have 22, only five more. But doesn't the cinquain read differently? Not sure? Look at this one:

The Warning

Just now,
Out of the strange
Still dusk . . . as strange, as still . . .
A white moth flew. Why am I grown
So cold?

ADELAIDE CRAPSEY

■ What does its pattern do?

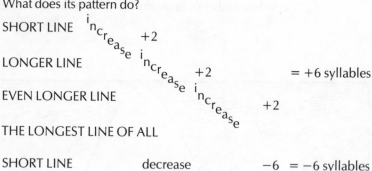

SHORT LINE increase +2

LONGER LINE increase +2 = +6 syllables

EVEN LONGER LINE increase +2

THE LONGEST LINE OF ALL

SHORT LINE decrease −6 = −6 syllables

A cinquain builds to a *climax* in line 4 with a sudden shrink-back in the last line.

■ The cinquain is also descriptive, but its subjects are often different from the haiku's. What did our haiku describe? What do the cinquains describe?

☐ In order to see this more clearly: try to rewrite the *Trafalgar Square* haiku as a cinquain, and *The Warning* cinquain as a haiku.

Is it possible? What has been gained or lost? The last line is short and unexpected, and so we see the rest of the poem in an entirely new way.

Adelaide Crapsey wrote a fine cinquain *November Night* and Geoffrey Holloway one called *Snowflake*. Both are in the anthology at the end of this chapter.

☐ Before reading them, write your own cinquain using one of their titles. Remember: make your last line your punchline!

If Adelaide Crapsey can invent a form, so can you.

haiku: 5—7—5
cinquain: 2—4—6—8—2

☐ Now invent your own 'haiquain': ?—????????.

If you can't think of a pattern try using your own or your school's
telephone number: zeroes can stand for a blank line or gap.

4 Shape Up

Words
Sentences
Poems

One leads to the other, but always? And do we always need lines?

Climax	**CL!MAX**
Alone	**ALON E**
Kiss	**KIS♥**

These are *shape-words*.

■ Can you see how a shape-word works? Explain these ones:

pregnant

LO⊔JCUT   EXXTRA

cockeysd

ʎOGA

These are all by Robert Carola. In the anthology at the end of the
chapter are six more: 'lift', 'balloon', 'astigmatism' (find out what this
word means), 'nonconformist', 'quicksand', 'incomplete'.

☐ Make them into shape-words, then compare yours with Robert
   Carola's. No cheating!

Our shape-words are in black print, but colours, crayons, and other
drawing instruments are ideal.

☐ Try 'HOT' in red, 'COLD' in blue. What about 'cracked', 'broken',
   'mirror', 'cuddly'? Now think of your own shape-words.

■ Look at this poem: not words, but a letter! Guess the title. (The answer is on page 22.)

☐ For how many other letters of the alphabet can you devise poems?

The evening star, a punctual gem, shines like a rajah's diadem.

Quite pretty! But let's improve its shape:

The evening star, a punctual gem,
Shines like a rajah's diadem

How many syllables are there in each line? Better still, it could be a *shape-sentence*:

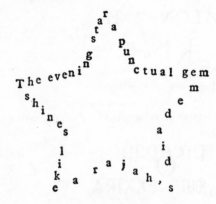

Immediately eye-catching.
It is by Apollinaire.

☐ Now you try this other sentence:

My heart the same as a flame upside down.

See the end of the chapter for Apollinaire's version.

☐ Try these sentences – change them into shape-sentences:

The necklace connects you to me
The enormous cigar burns
Puddles ooze everywhere
Needles and pins prick

If this is too easy, add an extra line: e.g.

The necklace connects you to me,
Together is what we want to be!

Snowflake

Snowflake,
bride of heaven,
your nuptial furlough's through.
You must come to earth. And, darling —
earth burns.

GEOFFREY HOLLOWAY

ROBERT CAROLA

I always eat peas with honey,
I've done it all my life,
They do taste kind of funny,
But it keeps them on the knife.

ANON

Days

What are days for?
Days are where we live.
They come, they wake us
Time and time over.
They are to be happy in:
Where can we live but days?
Ah, solving that question
Brings the priest and the doctor
In their long coats
Running over the fields.

PHILIP LARKIN

MANGO CHUTNEY

There's Something Sad

There's something sad
about the glass
with lipstick on its mouth
that's pointed at and given back
to the waitress in disgust

Like the girl with the hair-lip
whom
no one
wants
to
kiss.

ROGER MCGOUGH

Haiku

a green breeze dances
my washing dry. Smell of spring
in the airing cupboard

PATRICIA POGSON

November Night

Listen . . .
With faint dry sound,
Like steps of passing ghosts,
The leaves, frost-crisped, break from the trees
And fall.

ADELAIDE CRAPSEY

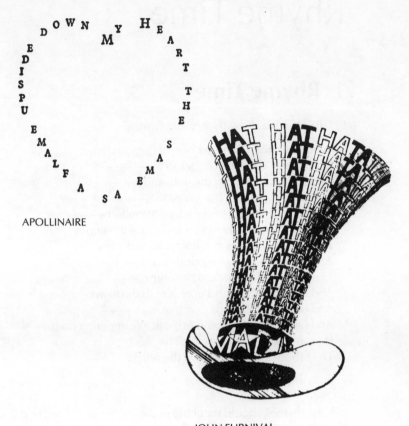

APOLLINAIRE

JOHN FURNIVAL

ENDPIECE: Poet's Chop-Suey

☐ Take your own poem, and write out each line on a small, separate piece of paper. Distribute the individual lines to as many others as possible.

☐ You will receive lines from several others. Write a poem using your new lines. You may simply put the lines in an order, but if this doesn't make sense, rearrange some of the words in the lines. Try to keep all the words you are given – but, if necessary, you may make small changes.

Rhyme Time

1 Rhyme Time

☐ Fill in the blanks with rhyming words:

When midnight comes a host of dogs and men
Go out and track the badger to his ———
And put a sack within the hole and lye
Till the old grunting badger passes ———
He comes and hears they let the strongest ———
The old fox hears the noise and drops the goose
The poacher shoots and hurrys from the cry
And the old hare half wounded buzzes bye
They get a forked stick to bear him ———
And clapt the dogs and bore him to the town
And bait him all the day with many ———
And laugh and shout and fright the scampering hogs
He runs along and bites at all he meets
They shout and hollo down the noisey ———

from JOHN CLARE's *The Badger*

Your rhymes should naturally make each pair of lines end with the
same sound.

☐ List as many rhymes as you can think of for these words:

      eat   blue   ate   moon

☐ You can often, but not always, find rhyme in poetry. Use the rhyme words you have just listed to write your own poem.

George Herbert wrote:

The Call

Come, my Way, my Truth, my Life:
Such a Way, as gives us breath:
Such a Truth, as ends all strife:
Such a Life, as killeth death.

Come, my Light, my Feast, my Strength:
Such a Light, as shows a feast:
Such a Feast, as mends in length:
Such a Strength, as makes his guest.

Come my Joy, my Love, my Heart:
Such a Joy, as none can move:
Such a Love, as none can part:
Such a Heart, as joys in love.

■ Read this poem through two or three times. Discuss the effect of the rhymes.

There are two peculiar rhymes in the poem; which are they? All the other rhymes are called *perfect* rhymes. Look at these:

      love   dove   glove   move

      have   grave   wave   rave

      now   low   cow   sow

■ Which is the odd rhyme out in each line – the *eye rhyme*? Can you give some more examples?

Eye-rhymes can be very useful because they can break up the monotony of perfect rhyme. Think about John Clare's *The Badger* – aren't the rhymes just a little too obvious? Herbert ends *The Call* by breaking the pattern of sound but keeping the pattern of rhyme. This keeps us interested. Rhyme helps us memorise lines, and gives poetry its form.

■ Look again at the rhymes in *The Badger* and *The Call*. Remember how in *The Badger* the rhyme was always in the next line. Where is the rhyme in *The Call*?

☐ Find three more rhymes for 'day' (a^1, a^2 and a^3) and 'bed' (b^1, b^2 and b^3). Use these rhymes to write a poem in two parts. The first part rhymes like *The Badger*:

_____	day
_____	a^1
_____	bed
_____	b^1

but the second is like *The Call*:

_____	a^2
_____	b^2
_____	a^3
_____	b^3

2 Drat That Hat: The Position of Rhyme

Poetry can surprise:

The Double Knock

Rat-tat it went upon the lion's chin;
'That hat, I know it!' cried the joyful girl;
'Summer's it is, I know him by his knock;
Comers like him are welcome as the day!
Lizzy! go down and open the street-door;
Busy I am to any one but *him*.
Know him you must – he has been often here;
Show him upstairs, and tell him I'm alone.'

THOMAS HOOD

■ Look closely – what's surprising? Re-read the poem, if necessary aloud.
Rhyme isn't just for the end of the line, is it? Though it can be: let's rewrite the Thomas Hood with rhymes at the end of lines as well.

Rat-tat it went upon the lion's chin;
'That hat – I'd better let its owner in;
Summer's it is, I know him by his knock;
Comers like him have funny ears like Spock!
Lizzy! . . .

☐ Try to complete the last four lines.

You can rhyme two start words
You can rhyme two end words
You can rhyme the first and last word in a line

☐ Where else can you rhyme? If you can think of another place for rhymes write out some lines with the pattern.

☐ Now read this section from *The Rime of the Ancient Mariner*. Pick out the lines where there is a new pattern of rhyme.

From *The Rime of the Ancient Mariner*

And I had done a hellish thing,
And it would work 'em woe:
For all averred, I had killed the bird
That made the breeze to blow.
Ah wretch! said they, the bird to slay,
That made the breeze to blow!

Nor dim nor red, like God's own head,
The glorious Sun uprist:
Then all averred, I had killed the bird
That brought the fog and mist.
'Twas right, said they, such birds to slay,
That bring the fog and mist.

The fair breeze blew, the white foam flew,
The furrow followed free;
We were the first that ever burst
Into that silent sea.

Down dropt the breeze, the sails dropt down,
'Twas sad as sad could be;
And we did speak only to break
The silence of the sea!

SAMUEL TAYLOR COLERIDGE

Make sure you read this out aloud. *The Ancient Mariner* is about a mysterious curse that comes on a man who kills an innocent bird, the Albatross.

■ Line 3 of the first stanza has the new rhyme pattern. What is it?

Which two words rhyme? Now look at line 5 – which two words rhyme? Pick out the other lines that rhyme in the middle of the line: this is called *internal rhyme*.

☐ In the last stanza there is an internal *eye rhyme* too. Can you spot it?

Rhymes have the effect of emphasising certain words; they also reinforce the poem's rhythm, with the rhymes ringing out like a chant.

☐ All together, read out these verses of *The Rime of the Ancient Mariner*, like a chorus.

■ Which of the rhyme patterns we've met – start, end and internal – do you find most effective to read, or to write? Discuss your reasons.

☐ Now have fun – use rhymes in as many different positions as you can!

3 Prepocerous Rhinoceroses: Comic Rhymes

☐ Find rhymes for:

eerier   atrocious   general   uniform   historical

Not so easy! Words with one syllable often have rhymes. But words of many syllables can be awkward to rhyme. This can be an advantage:

The Firefly

The firefly's flame
Is something for which science has no name.
I can think of nothing eerier
Than flying around with an unidentified red glow on a person's
    posterior.

OGDEN NASH

This mother has a well-developed son:

From Don Juan

54
Young Juan now was sixteen years of age,
    Tall, handsome, slender, but well knit: he seemed
Active, though not so sprightly, as a page;
    And everybody but his mother deemed
Him almost man; but she flew in a rage
    And bit her lips (for else she might have screamed)
If any said so, for to be precocious
Was in her eyes a thing the most atrocious.

LORD BYRON

☐ Read this as fast as you can:

Major-General

I am the very model of a modern Major-General,
I've information vegetable, animal, and mineral,
I know the kings of England, and I quote the fights historical,
From Marathon to Waterloo, in order categorical;
I'm very well acquainted too with matters mathematical,
I understand equations, both the simple and quadratical,

About binomial theorem I'm teeming with a lot o' news —
With many cheerful facts about the square of the hypotenuse,
I'm very good at integral and differential calculus,
I know the scientific names of beings animalculous;
In short, in matters vegetable, animal, and mineral,
I am the very model of a modern Major-General.
I know our mythic history, King Arthur's and Sir Caradoc's,
I answer hard acrostics, I've a pretty taste for paradox,
I quote in elegiacs all the crimes of Heliogabalus,
In conics I can floor peculiarities parabolous,
I can tell undoubted Raphaels from Gerard Dows and Zoffanies,
I know the croaking chorus from the Frogs of Aristophanes,
Then I can hum a fugue of which I've heard the music's din afore,
And whistle all the airs from that infernal nonsense 'Pinafore',
Then I can write a washing bill in Babylonic cuneiform,
And tell you every detail of Caractacus's uniform;
In short, in matters vegetable, animal, and mineral,
I am the very model of a modern Major-General.

W.S. GILBERT

How fast did you read it? Check the dictionary for pronunciation! Now try again, really fast.

☐ Who can read it the fastest? There are 24 lines: let each person in the group read one line, and again build up speed in the reading.

■ What is the effect of rhyming long words compared with short ones? Discuss.

Sometimes the rhyme has to be made to fit:

The Rhinoceros

The rhino is a homely beast,
For human eyes he's not a feast,
But you and I will never know
Why nature chose to make him so.
Farewell, farewell, you old rhinoceros,
I'll stare at something less prepocerous!

OGDEN NASH

Here are some homely and less homely beasts: parakeet, pottoroo, platypus, hippopotamus, aardvark, giraffe, and zebra.

☐ Find rhymes for some of these creatures in your comic poem. If you have to, 'bend' the rhyme to make it fit!

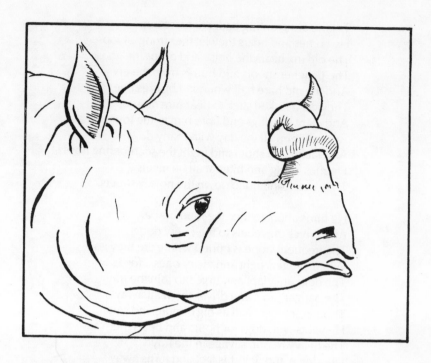

ANTHOLOGY 3

The Badger

The badger grunting on his woodland track
With shaggy hide and sharp nose scrowed with black
Roots in the bushes and the woods and makes
A great hugh burrow in the ferns and brakes
With nose on ground he runs an awkward pace
And anything will beat him in the race
The shepherds dog will run him to his den
Followed and hooted by the dogs and men
The woodman when the hunting comes about
Go round at night to stop the foxes out
And hurrying through the bushes ferns and brakes
Nor sees the many holes the badger makes
And often through the bushes to the chin
Breaks the old holes and tumbles headlong in.

When midnight comes a host of dogs and men
Go out and track the badger to his den
And put a sack within the hole and lye

Till the old grunting badger passes bye
He comes and hears they let the strongest loose
The old fox hears the noise and drops the goose
The poacher shoots and hurrys from the cry
And the old hare half wounded buzzes bye
They get a forked stick to bear him down
And clapt the dogs and bore him to the town
And bait him all the day with many dogs
And laugh and shout and fright the scampering hogs
He runs along and bites at all he meets
They shout and hollo down the noisey streets.

He turns about to face the loud uproar
And drives the rebels to their very doors
The frequent stone is hurled where ere they go
When badgers fight and every ones a foe
The dogs are clapt and urged to join the fray
The badger turns and drives them all away
Though scarcely half as big dimute and small
He fights with dogs for hours and beats them all
The heavy mastiff savage in the fray
Lies down and licks his feet and turns away
The bull dog knows his match and waxes cold
The badger grins and never leaves his hold
He drives the crowd and follows at their heels
And bites them through the drunkard swears and reels.

The frighted women takes the boys away
The blackguard laughs and hurrys on the fray
He tries to reach the woods an awkward race
But sticks and cudgels quickly stop the chace
He turns agen and drives the noisey crowd
And beats the many dogs in noises loud
He drives away and beats them every one
And then they loose them all and set them on
He falls as dead and kicked by boys and men
Then starts and grins and drives the crowd agen
Till kicked and torn and beaten out he lies
And leaves his hold and cackles groans and dies.

Some keep a baited badger tame as hog
And tame him till he follows like the dog
They urge him on like dogs and show fair play
He beats and scarcely wounded goes away
Lapt up as if asleep he scorns to fly
And siezes any dog that ventures nigh

Clapt like a dog he never bites the men
But worrys dogs and hurrys to his den
They let him out and turn a harrow down
And there he fights the host of all the town
He licks the patting hand and trys to play
And never trys to bite or run away
And runs away from noise in hollow trees
Burnt by the boys to get a swarm of bees.

JOHN CLARE

The Young Metaphysician

There was once a metaphysician
Who claimed that he didn't exist,
But when he explained his position
They exclaimed, 'Well, you'll never be missed!'

ANON

The Revenge

A BALLAD OF THE FLEET

1

At Flores in the Azores Sir Richard Grenville lay,
And a pinnace, like a flutter'd bird, came flying from far away:
'Spanish ships of war at sea! we have sighted fifty-three!'
Then sware Lord Thomas Howard: "Fore God I am no coward;
But I cannot meet them here, for my ships are out of gear,
And the half my men are sick. I must fly, but follow quick.
We are six ships of the line; can we fight with fifty-three?'

2

Then spake Sir Richard Grenville: 'I know you are no coward,
You fly them for a moment to fight with them again.
But I've ninety men and more that are lying sick ashore.
I should count myself the coward if I left them, my Lord Howard,
To these Inquisition dogs and the devildoms of Spain.'

3

So Lord Howard past away with five ships of war that day,
Till he melted like a cloud in the silent summer heaven;

But Sir Richard bore in hand all his sick men from the land
Very carefully and slow,
Men of Bideford in Devon,
And we laid them on the ballast down below;
For we brought them all aboard,
And they blest him in their pain, that they were not left to Spain,
To the thumbscrew and the stake, for the glory of the Lord.

4

He had only a hundred seamen to work the ship and to fight,
And he sailed away from Flores till the Spaniard came in sight,
With his huge sea-castles heaving upon the weather bow.
'Shall we fight or shall we fly?
Good Sir Richard, tell us now,
For to fight is but to die!
There'll be little of us left by the time this sun be set.'
And Sir Richard said again: 'We be all good English men.
Let us bang these dogs of Seville, the children of the devil,
For I never turn'd my back upon Don or devil yet.'

5

Sir Richard spoke and he laugh'd, and we roar'd a hurrah, and so
The little Revenge ran on sheer into the heart of the foe,
With her hundred fighters on deck, and her ninety sick below,
For half of their fleet to the right and half to the left were seen,
And the little Revenge ran on thro' the long sea-lane between.

6

Thousands of their soldiers look'd down from their decks and laugh'd,
Thousands of their seamen made mock at the mad little craft
Running on and on, till delay'd
By their mountain-like San Philip that, of fifteen hundred tons,
And up-shadowing high above us with her yawning tiers of guns,
Took the breath from our sails, and we stay'd.

7

And while now the great San Philip hung above us like a cloud
Whence the thunderbolt will fall
Long and loud,
Four galleons drew away
From the Spanish fleet that day,
And two upon the larboard and two upon the starboard lay,
And the battle-thunder broke from them all.

But anon the great San Philip, she bethought herself and went
Having that within her womb that had left her ill content;
And the rest they came aboard us, and they fought us hand to hand,
For a dozen times they came with their pikes and musqueteers,
And a dozen times we shook 'em off as a dog that shakes his ears
When he leaps from the water to the land.

9

And the sun went down, and the stars came out far over the summer
    sea,
But never a moment ceased the fight of the one and the fifty-three.
Ship after ship, the whole night long, their high-built galleons came,
Ship after ship, the whole night long, with her battle-thunder and
    flame;
Ship after ship, the whole night long, drew back with her dead and her
    shame.
For some were sunk and many were shatter'd, and so could fight us no
    more –
God of battles, was ever a battle like this in the world before?

10

For he said 'Fight on! fight on!'
Tho' his vessel was all but a wreck;
And it chanced that, when half of the short summer night was gone,
With a grisly wound to be drest he had left the deck,
But a bullet struck him that was dressing it suddenly dead,
And himself he was wounded again in the side and the head,
And he said 'Fight on! fight on!'

11

And the night went down, and the sun smiled out far over the summer
    sea,
And the Spanish fleet with broken sides lay round us all in a ring;
But they dared not touch us again, for they fear'd that we still could
    sting,
So they watch'd what the end would be.
And we had not fought them in vain,
But in perilous plight were we,
Seeing forty of our poor hundred were slain,
And half of the rest of us maim'd for life
In the crash of the cannonades and the desperate strife;
And the sick men down in the hold were most of them stark and cold,
And the pikes were all broken or bent, and the powder was all of it
    spent;

And the masts and the rigging were lying over the side;
But Sir Richard cried in his English pride,
'We have fought such a fight for a day and a night
As may never be fought again!
We have won great glory, my men!
And a day less or more
At sea or ashore,
We die – does it matter when?
Sink me the ship, Master Gunner – sink her, split her in twain!
Fall into the hands of God, not into the hands of Spain!'

12

And the gunner said 'Ay, ay,' but the seamen made reply:
'We have children, we have wives,
And the Lord hath spared our lives.
We will make the Spaniard promise, if we yield, to let us go;
We shall live to fight again and to strike another blow.'
And the lion there lay dying, and they yielded to the foe.

13

And the stately Spanish men to their flagship bore him then,
Where they laid him by the mast, old Sir Richard caught at last,
And they praised him to his face with their courtly foreign grace;
But he rose upon their decks, and he cried:
'I have fought for Queen and Faith like a valiant man and true;
I have only done my duty as a man is bound to do:
With a joyful spirit I Sir Richard Grenville die!'
And he fell upon their decks, and he died.

14

And they stared at the dead that had been so valiant and true,
And had holden the power and glory of Spain so cheap
That he dared her with one little ship and his English few;
Was he devil or man? He was devil for aught they knew,
But they sank his body with honour down into the deep,
And they mann'd the Revenge with a swarthier alien crew,
And away she sail'd with her loss and long'd for her own;
When a wind from the lands they had ruin'd awoke from sleep,
And the water began to heave and the weather to moan,
And or ever that evening ended a great gale blew,
And a wave like the wave that is raised by an earthquake grew,
Till it smote on their hulls and their sails and their masts and their flags,

And the whole sea plunged and fell on the shot-shatter'd navy of
    Spain,
And the little Revenge herself went down by the island crags
To be lost evermore in the main.

LORD TENNYSON

ENDPIECE: Library Project

Poetry usually comes from experience. The lives of poets, then, can be
very interesting, and perhaps help us appreciate their poetry more.

☐ Use your library to find out about a famous poet.
    You could choose S.T. Coleridge, if you enjoyed *The Ancient
Mariner*. When was he born? When did he die? Can you find his
wife's name? Which one of his sons was also a poet? And who was
his famous poet friend?
    More important than these questions, can you name three or four
of his most famous poems? Read one of them and illustrate it.
    Kubla Khan is one of his great poems. There is a story about the
writing of this poem — find out what it is. Write a short story called
The Man from Porlock. Who was Kubla Khan?

Choosing Words

1 Choosing the Right Word

*Alfred
Lord Tennyson*

One of these poems is by Lord Tennyson. One isn't.

The Eagle

He clasps the crag with crooked hands,
Close to the sun in lonely lands,
Ring'd with the azure world he stands.

The wrinkled sea beneath him crawls;
He watches from his mountain walls,
And like a thunderbolt he falls.

The Eagle

He hangs on the cliff with twisted feet,
Next to the sun all by himself,
Surrounded by blue sky, he hovers.

The lumpy sea beneath him sloshes about a bit;
He peeps out from his cosy nest,
And like a half a brick he falls.

Find the *real* Tennyson poem!

■ What are the differences between the two poems?

Probably the first thing you noticed about the second version was
that it *sounded* wrong. Why is this?

■ Look at these pairs of words. Discuss which is the most suitable and
why. Think about sound as well as meaning.

Tennyson	not Tennyson
clasps	hangs on
crag	cliff
crooked	twisted
hands	feet
lonely	by himself
stands	hovers
wrinkled	lumpy
crawls	sloshes about a bit
thunderbolt	half a brick

Discuss any other ways in which the non-Tennyson poem is not as
good as the real one.

A good dictionary is a vital tool for the writer, and here is a chance for
you to use yours! In this poem Wes Magee has selected his words not
only for meaning, but also because the first letters of each word form
the alphabet.

An A–Z of Headlines

Atomic Blast Cripples Doncaster
Excitable Foreman Garrottes Hooligans
Injured Judge's Kidney Lost
Mad Nun Ousts Pope
Queen Rewrites Shakespeare's Tragedies
Ubiquitous Venusian Worships Xylophone
Yak Zooms

WES MAGEE

☐ Use your dictionary to write your own alphabet poem. You could
look up any words you don't know in the Wes Magee poem at the
same time.

2 Words and Meanings

The English language has many words that mean almost – but not quite – the same thing. 'Having your employment terminated' isn't quite the same thing as 'getting the sack' – it's more polite! The end result is the same, however.

Think now about *wetness*.

          soused
     humid   damp
  awash   saturated
              wet
  watery   soaked
        sodden   sopping
      moist   drenched

All of these words are connected with wetness, but some differ in meaning; 'humid', for example, refers to the air.

■ Discuss the different meanings of these words. You might be able to put them in order of wetness.

Robert Southey, in his poem *The Cataract of Lodore,* tried to come up with as many words as he could to describe the sound and movement of water rushing down a cascade. Here is an extract from that poem:

From *The Cataract of Lodore*

The cataract strong
Then plunges along,
Striking and raging
As if a way waging
Its caverns and rocks among:
Rising and leaping,
Sinking and creeping,
Swelling and sweeping,
Showering and springing,
Flying and flinging,
Writhing and ringing,
Eddying and whisking,
Spouting and frisking,
Turning and twisting,
Around and around
With endless rebound!
Smiting and fighting,
A sight to delight in;
Confounding, astounding,

Dizzying and deafening the ear with its sound.
Dividing and gliding and sliding,
And falling and brawling and sprawling,
And driving and riving and striving,
And sprinkling and twinkling and wrinkling,
And sounding and bounding and rounding,
And bubbling and troubling and doubling,
And grumbling and rumbling and tumbling,
And clattering and battering and shattering;
Retreating and beating and meeting and sheeting,
Delaying and straying and playing and spraying,
Advancing and prancing and glancing and dancing,
Recoiling, turmoiling and toiling and boiling,
And gleaming and streaming and steaming and beaming,
And rushing and flushing and brushing and gushing,
And flapping and rapping and clapping and slapping,
And curling and whirling and purling and twirling,
And thumping and plumping and bumping and jumping,
And dashing and flashing and splashing and clashing;
And so never ending, but always descending,
Sounds and motions for ever and ever are blending,
All at once and all o'er, with a mighty uproar,
And this way the water comes down at Lodore.

ROBERT SOUTHEY

■ Pick out some of the interesting words in *The Cataract of Lodore*. Try to picture what sort of movement or sound is being described. Here are some you might discuss:

brawling	chattering
sprawling	sheeting
wrinkling	brushing
troubling	plumping
grumbling	beaming

☐ Think of as many 'human voice' words as you can: 'whispering', 'shouting', and so on. Try to put them in order of *loudness*. Are some of your words different in meaning? What about 'singing', for instance?

☐ Try to write a 'wordlist' poem like *The Cataract of Lodore*. Suitable subjects could be a tidal wave, an earthquake, an avalanche, a battle, or a huge rock rolling down a mountain.

3 Making New Words

Stuck for a word? Make one up! Here is a made-up word:

stroogling

Come up with a meaning for it!
Made-up words are properly called *neologisms,* and the point about these words is that readers do not know what they mean unless you suggest their meaning. Here is a poem made up entirely of neologisms.

Suckerslick

Sluckwoozy, sloated suckerslick
Slapperslumping.

SLAT!

   Swurgled, mushwacked,
Suckerslick snackered swetly,

      Soggled.

MANGO CHUTNEY

■ What do you think this poem is about?

Well, you can't be too sure, but probably something rather slimy has met with an unfortunate accident!

Jabberwocky

'Twas brillig, and the slithy toves
Did gyre and gimble in the wabe;
All mimsy were the borogroves,
And the mome raths outgrabe.

'Beware the Jabberwock, my son!
The jaws that bite, the claws that catch!
Beware the Jubjub bird and shun
The frumious Bandersnatch!'

He took his vorpal sword in hand;
Long time the manxome foe he sought –
So rested he by the Tumtum tree,
And stood awhile in thought.

And as in uffish thought he stood,
The Jabberwock, with eyes of flame,
Came whiffling through the tulgey wood,
And burbled as it came!

One, two! One, two! And through and through
The vorpal blade went snicker-snack!
He left it dead, and with its head
He went galumphing back.

'And hast thou slain the Jabberwock?
Come to my arms, my beamish boy!
O frabjous day! Callooh! Callay!'
He chortled in his joy.

'Twas brillig, and the slithy toves
Did gyre and gimble in the wabe;
All mimsy were the borogroves,
And the mome raths outgrabe.

LEWIS CARROLL

This poem has a number of neologisms in it, and Humpty Dumpty explains some of them for us (see below). A *portmanteau word* is a special type of neologism. It is made by combining two existing words:

motel = motor hotel

■ Find portmanteau words in *Jabberwocky* made from these words:

lithe & slimy
galloping & triumphant
chuckled & snorted

From *Through the Looking-Glass*

'Twas brillig, and the slithy toves
   Did gyre and gimble in the wabe:
All mimsy were the borogoves,
   And the mome raths outgrabe.

'That's enough to begin with,' Humpty Dumpty interrupted: 'there are plenty of hard words there. "*Brillig*" means four o'clock in the afternoon – the time when you begin *broiling* things for dinner.'
   'That'll do very well,' said Alice: 'and "*slithy*"?'
   'Well, "*slithy*" means "lithe and slimy." "Lithe" is the same as "active." You see it's like a portmanteau – there are two meanings packed up into one word.'
   'I see it now,' Alice remarked thoughtfully: 'and what are "*toves*"?'
   'Well, "*toves*" are something like badgers – they're something like lizards – and they're something like corkscrews.'
   'They must be very curious-looking creatures.'
   'They are that,' said Humpty Dumpty: 'also they make their nests under sun-dials – also they live on cheese.'
   'And what's to "*gyre*" and to "*gimble*"?'
   'To "*gyre*" is to go round and round like a gyroscope. To "*gimble*" is to make holes like a gimblet.'
   'And "*the wabe*" is the grass-plot round a sundial, I suppose?' said Alice, surprised at her own ingenuity.
   'Of course it is. It's called "*wabe*," you know, because it goes a long way before it, and a long way behind it –'
   'And a long way beyond it on each side,' Alice added.
   'Exactly so. Well then, "*mimsy*" is "flimsy and miserable" (there's another portmanteau for you). And a "*borogove*" is a thin shabby-looking bird with its feathers sticking out all round – something like a live mop.'
   'And then "*mome raths*"?' said Alice. 'I'm afraid I'm giving you a great deal of trouble.'
   'Well, a "*rath*" is a sort of green pig: but "*mome*" I'm not certain about. I think it's short for "from home" – meaning that they'd lost

their way, you know.'

'And what does "*outgrabe*" mean?'

'Well, "*outgribing*" is something between bellowing and whistling, with a kind of sneeze in the middle; however you'll hear it done, maybe – down in the wood yonder – and, when you've once heard it, you'll be *quite* content.'

LEWIS CARROLL

■ What do *you* think these words mean: 'frumious', 'vorpal', 'manxome', 'uffish' and 'beamish'?

☐ Write a poem like *Suckerslick* that is made up entirely of neologisms.

And he grinned almost from ear to ear . . . .

4 Dialect

A *dialect* is a local version of a language. It is different from other versions in the way it is pronounced and in the words used. English is a very widespread language, but in different countries, and in different areas of countries, it is used differently.

Try to guess what this stanza is about. It is part of a poem by Robert Burns, written in Scottish dialect (called 'Scots').

My curse upon your venom'd stang,
That shoots my tortured gums alang;
And thro' my lugs gies monie a twang,
  Wi' gnawing vengeance;
Tearing my nerves wi' bitter pang,
  Like racking engines!

The answer is on page 48.

Barry Heath lives in the county of Nottingham, which is in the English Midlands. This poem has only one dialect word in it; 'tab' means 'ear'. If you don't understand the poem, try reading it out loud!

First Day at School

it wurorribul m'fost
day a schooil
memate jeff flewit
went wime
an teacha wunt lerrus
sit next tureachother

went shiwent aht
cockut class cumup
t'me
ansed, 'AH canfaityo
cahnt ah?'
an ah sed eecudnt
an ee sed ee cud
an ah sed ee cuddent
an eeit me
so ah itim back just
as teacha cumin

shipicked up that
stick as y'point
at bord'we
an crackt m'ovver
edweeit
an sed, 'Widontav
ooligunsere.'

so ah went omm at
playtime an towd
memam
an memam took meback
t'school agen
owdin metab

☐ Read the poem *Insec' Lesson* on page 50. This poem is written in West Indian dialect. Retell the poem in your own dialect; remember, 'Standard English' is a special sort of dialect! If you have local words for any of the things described in the poem, use them.

Robert Burns's poem
The poem by Robert Burns, 'My curse upon your venom'd stang', is about toothache.

ANTHOLOGY 4

From *The Schooner*

Just mark that schooner westward far at sea –
   'Tis but an hour ago
When she was lying hoggish at the quay,
   And men ran to and fro,
And tugged, and stamped, and shoved, and pushed, and swore,
And ever and anon, with crapulous glee,
Grinned homage to viragoes on the shore.

So to the jetty gradual she was hauled:
   The one the tiller took,
And chewed, and spat upon his hand, and bawled;
   And one the canvas shook
Forth like a mouldy bat; and one, with nods
And smiles, lay on the bowsprit-end, and called
And cursed the Harbour-master by his gods.

And, rotten from the gunwale to the keel,
   Rat-riddled, bilge-bestank,
Slime-slobbered, horrible, I saw her reel,
   And drag her oozy flank,
And sprawl among the deft young waves, that laughed,
And leapt, and turned in many a sportive wheel,
As she thumped onward with her lumbering draught.

T.E. BROWN

Chilly Dovebber with his boadigg blast
Dow cubs add strips the bedow add the lawd,
Eved October's suddy days are past —
Add Subber's gawd!

I kdow dot what it is to which I cligg
That stirs to sogg add sorrow, yet I trust
That still I sigg, but as the liddets sigg —
Because I bust.

Add now, farewell to roses add to birds,
To larded fields and tigkligg streablets eke;
Farewell to all articulated words
I fain would speak.

Farewell, by cherished strolliggs od the sward,
Greed glades and forest shades, farewell to you;
With sorrowing heart I, wretched add forlord,
Bid you — achew!!!

ANON

Eachie, peachie, pearie, plum,
Throw the tatties up the lum.
Santa Claus got one on the bum,
Eachie, peachie, pearie, plum.

ANON

Did you ever, ever, ever,
In your leaf, life, loaf,
See the deevel, divil, dovol,
Kiss his weef, wife, woaf?
No, I never, never, never,
In my leaf, life, loaf,
Saw the deevel, divil, dovol,
Kiss his weef, wife, woaf.

ANON

From *Insec' Lesson*

Todder nite mi a watch one program,
Yuh did watch it to Miss Vie?
De one wid de whole heap o'ants an'bug,
Mi couldn' believe mi yeye

When mi see ow de ants dem lib
An hep out one anedda,
So much hundred tousan ants
Dey wuk an' pull togedda.

De mooma ants she big an fat
So she liddung lay egg all day.
De solja ants tan up guard de door,
Mek sure no enemy no come dem way.

De worka ants a de bessis one,
Dem always wuk togedda
Fi feed de queen, an store de eggs,
An wash dem likkle bredda.

Some go out fi gadda food
Fi feed dose in de nes'
Some a dig hole fi mek new room
An some clean up de mess.

I' please mi fi see ow de ants dem pull,
An try fi get tings done,
Dem wuk an eat an sleep togedda
An a not even dem one.

Far mi see whole heap o' odda insect
Wasp, bug an fly an bee,
All a wuk togedda
Ina perfec' harmony.

VALERIE BLOOM

☐ Try sending your poetry for publication outside the school. (You might like to try The Schools' Poetry Association, 27 Pennington Close, Colden Common, Nr. Winchester, Hants.) But remember to keep a copy!

☐ Write to another school in your area. Offer to exchange poems.

☐ Write to your local radio station or newspaper, offering them a *small* selection of your poems. If you make your poems topical, there is more chance of their being accepted. Don't be upset if you are rejected. As the poet Brian Hinton says,

And finally, don't despair — even cuddly Pam Ayres was
told to give up; Gerry Hopkins died unread. They'll
suffer when they realize, crawling on bent knees. So
welcome to heartbreak, now you're a player.

'Keep trying' should be your motto!

Pictures in Words

1 Strange Comparisons

The Sea

The sea is a hungry dog,
Giant and grey.
He rolls on the beach all day.
With his clashing teeth and shaggy jaws
Hour upon hour he gnaws
The rumbling, tumbling stones,
And 'Bones, bones, bones, bones!'
The giant sea-dog moans,
Licking his greasy paws.

And when the night wind roars
And the moon rocks in the stormy cloud,
He bounds to his feet and snuffs and sniffs,
Shaking his wet sides over the cliffs,
And howls and hollos long and loud.

But on quiet days of May or June,
When even the grasses on the dune
Play no more their reedy tune,
With his head between his paws
He lies on the sandy shores,
So quiet, so quiet, he scarcely snores.

JAMES REEVES

The sea? This poem seems to tell us more about a dog! James Reeves is
telling us that, in some ways, the sea is *like* a dog.

■ Like a dog? How can that be? See if you can add to this table:

sea	dog
'gnaws' pebbles	gnaws bones
has 'moods'	
	can be dangerous!

■ Try the poem the other way round. If it was called *The Dog is a Hungry Sea*, would it still make sense?

James Reeves was making a surprising comparison between two different things. What do you think of *this* comparison?

The light is like a spider . . .

How on earth can light be like a spider? Here is another table for you to add to, but this time it shows differences.

spider	light
dark	the opposite of dark
creepy	cheerful
eight legs	no legs!

Now let's read the poem and see why light *is* like a spider!

Light

The light is like a spider.
It crawls over the water.
It crawls over the edge of the snow.
It crawls under your eyelids
And spreads its webs there –
Its two webs.

WALLACE STEVENS

Light is like a spider in the way it gradually creeps up on us in the morning. The idea of spiders creeping under our eyelids is not very pleasant!

☐ Now think of a comparison of your own. Write a list. Everyone should be able to think of at least two! Here are some to start you off.

Fire is a ravenous tiger
The wind is a howling wolf
Snow is . . .
Snails . . .

☐ Now is your chance to use one of the comparisons from your list in a poem of your own. You don't have to use the ones *you* thought of – share your ideas.

2 Discovering Similes

How do you feel about another poetry lesson? Sick as a parrot? Flat as a pancake? Keen as mustard? What do you think of this book so far? Dull as ditchwater? Dry as dust? Like a damp squib?

These well-known sayings are *comparisons,* like the ones we met in the last section. The trouble with these sayings is that they are so well known that they don't say anything new. Try to avoid them in your writing. You don't want to send your readers to sleep!

Now look out for fresh comparisons.

Autumn

A touch of cold in the Autumn night —
I walked abroad,
And saw the ruddy moon lean over a hedge
Like a red-faced farmer.
I did not stop to speak, but nodded,
And round about were the wistful stars
With white faces like town children.

T.E. HULME

■ Do you think the moon can really be compared with a red-faced farmer looking over a hedge? Why might town children be compared with stars?

Comparisons that use the words 'like' or 'as' are called *similes* (pronounced 'sim-e-lees'). We started this section with some; here are some more.

> Like two peas in a pod
> Red as a beetroot
> Light is like a spider
> The moon is like a red-faced farmer

☐ On the page opposite there is a *simile picture*. These are fun to do. You can add similes to a picture drawn by someone else, or you could draw your own.

☐ Choose something to describe, and make up as many similes as you can. Here is an example.

> **Tree**
> As tall as a lighthouse
> It bends like a tall ship in a storm
> Branches reach out like cranes
> Bark like an elephant's hide

Don't stop at four! You will think of the obvious ideas first, then, as you think really hard, more interesting ideas will come. Your list of similes will not be a poem, but you will be able to use some of them in a poem later.

3 Discovering Metaphors

The Beach

The beach is a quarter of golden fruit,
A soft ripe melon
Sliced to a half-moon curve,
Having a thick green rind
Of jungle growth;
And the sea devours it
With its sharp
White teeth.

WILLIAM HART-SMITH

The beach – a delicious slice of melon. The sea – an animal eating the melon!

■ Why do you think the whiteness of the animal's teeth is mentioned?

■ What is the difference in the way these two comparisons are made?

The beach *is* a quarter of golden fruit.
The light is *like* a spider.

William Hart-Smith does not use the word 'like': he says that the beach *is* a quarter of fruit. He does not say 'The waves were as sharp and white as an animal's teeth': he tells us that the sea really does have teeth! This is not true, of course. The poet is making a comparison.

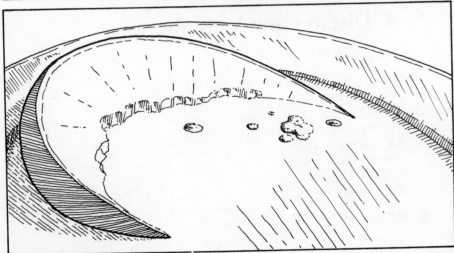

☐ Here is another 'comparison' picture. Now write the poem! Do not use 'as' or 'like'.

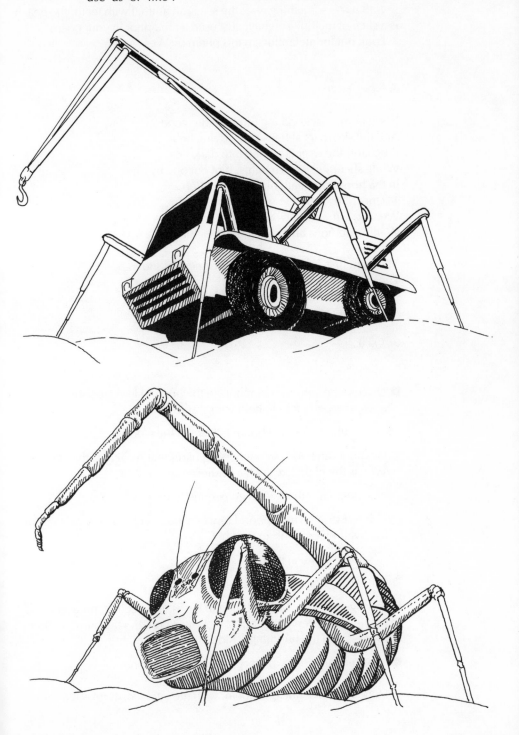

We can now meet a new word, *metaphor* (pronounced 'met-a-for'). A *simile* says that the thing described is *like* something else. A metaphor says that it *is* something else: the sea is an animal with teeth, the beach is a slice of melon. You have just used a metaphor in your poem.

Look out for metaphors in this poem by Wes Magee.

A New Year

Night comes jackbooting through the wood
And the sky roars at trees and a dying light.
Pregnant, the river is gulped into darkness
While sheep, like town lights, blot out one by one.
In the house, beneath blanketing thatch,
Twenty of us gather to see the new year in.
We talk; wine runs away with itself;
Wailing demons are trapped up the chimney.

Midnight first-foots with a bombardment of snow.
The wind is celebrating madly.
Owls rattle in barns as we clasp hands
And another year is born in a blitz of stars.

WES MAGEE

■ Discuss the various metaphors in the poem. Here are some questions and ideas to help your discussion.

Night comes jackbooting through the wood . . .

Jackboots are worn by soldiers, in particular by very ruthless ones. Why is the night like such a soldier?

Pregnant, the river is gulped into darkness . . .

This is a strange metaphor! How can the river be pregnant? What are the 'wailing demons' in the chimney?

Owls rattle in barns . . .

Why does Wes Magee use this metaphor?

Wes Magee writes: 'Owls rattling in barns' is a 'feeling' phrase. In reality it means very little, but somehow it conveys the barn's echoing emptiness and the huddling, cold nature of the night.'

■ Are there any more military metaphors in this poem?

☐ Here is the first line of a poem, with the vital words missing!

The ___ is a ___ of ___

Fill in the missing words, then finish the poem.

4 Images

These two short poems present a single picture or *image*.

In a Station of the Metro

The apparition of these faces in the crowd;
Petals on a wet, black bough.

EZRA POUND

This Smoky Winter Morning

This smoky winter morning —
do not despise the green jewel shining among the twigs
because it is a traffic light.

CHARLES REZNIKOFF

■ What did the poets actually see?

■ What comparison did they make?

People coming out of an underground railway station	Flower petals stuck on the wet black branch of a tree
Green traffic light glowing through the fog	A green jewel

This is one of the things that writers do: they see things more imaginatively than other people!

☐ Now try this. Find some very ordinary objects and try to picture them in an unusual way. You might use books, pens and rubbers, for instance; think of these items on a much larger scale. What might your chewed pen be? A rocket? What about that pencil-case? Produce a table like the one above for your 'ordinary objects'.

You are going to write some 'instant' poems. Firstly, you will need a good simile; you should find one in the work you have done on this chapter. Here is an example:

Goldfish in a pool are like gold pennies spilt from a wreck.

If we imitate *In a Station of the Metro* we get:

Goldfish

Goldfish in a pool;
Golden pennies spilt from a wreck.

Here is another:

A tall tree;
Bending like a ship's mast in a storm.

☐ Try out some of your own, then illustrate them.
You've not used rhyme or rhythm this time; but you have used *imagery* to create a poem.

A Windy Day

This wind brings all dead things to life,
Branches that lash the air like whips
And dead leaves rolling in a hurry
Or peering in a rabbits' bury
Or trying to push down a tree;
Gates that fly open to the wind
And close again behind,
And fields that are a flowing sea
And make the cattle look like ships;

Straws glistening and stiff
Lying on air as on a shelf
And pond that leaps to leave itself;
And feathers too that rise and float,
Each feather changed into a bird,
And line-hung sheets that crack and strain;
Even the sun-greened coat,
That through so many winds has served,
The scarecrow struggles to put on again.

ANDREW YOUNG

Fetching Cows

The black one, last as usual, swings her head
And coils a black tongue round a grass-tuft. I
Watch her soft weight come down, her slip feet spread.

In front, the others swing and slouch; they roll
Their great Greek eyes and breathe out milky gusts
From muzzles black and shiny as wet coal.

The collie trots, bored, at my heels, then plops
Into the ditch. The sea makes a tired sound
That's always stopping though it never stops.

A haycart squats prickeared against the sky.
Hay breath and milk breath. Far out in the west
The wrecked sun founders though its colours fly.

64

The collie's bored. There's nothing to control . . .
The black cow is two native carriers
Bringing its belly home, slung from a pole.

NORMAN MACCAIG

Robin

As heavy snow falls
he's a red-vested Batman
on the garden fence.

WES MAGEE

About an Excavation

About an excavation
a flock of bright red lanterns

has settled.

CHARLES REZNIKOFF

Storm in the forest;
The whispering of a thousand bellydancers!

HUGH COCHRANE

ENDPIECE: The Mini-Magazine

☐ Get some sheets of paper or card, folded down the middle, and you
have a magazine ready for write-up or paste-up. This can be a
permanent record of the highlights of your work.

Information that might be included: reviews of readings, new
'chop-suey' poems, news on Coleridge, replies to your letters,
including any work submitted (from, for example, another school),
and, of course, copies of your best poems, and the best produced in
your class. You can also add information from anywhere else –
perhaps a newspaper cutting on poetry.

Writing a Poem

1 Getting Started

Writing a poem is easy. Writing a *good* poem is hard work!
These are the simplest stages in writing a poem.
- The first idea
- Getting something down
- Getting it right
- Knowing when it is finished

The first idea
How do we get it? Perhaps from:

A visit to a particular place
Relationships with other people
An unexpected incident
Reading books, seeing films, listening to music
Looking at pictures
Treasured objects
Powerful personal feelings
Problems faced by the writer

There is another way that a poem might start. A teacher might ask you to produce one! Luckily, we all have memories, and we can use them to write about things from this list.

☐ Think back over your recent past. Jot down *three* things that might be good subjects for poems. What details would you include? Don't lose your notes!

Getting something down
Here is a way of making that difficult first move, getting something down on paper. It's called . . .

The Big Scribble

The idea is to scribble down as many words, phrases and ideas as you can think of, even if they are only remotely connected with what you are writing about. Much of what you write you will not use, but beginning like this is good because
- it gets you started
- it gets all the dull ideas out of the way
- it gives you plenty to work on

■ Imagine now that someone was asked to write a poem about walking through a wood at night. Shown opposite is a page from this person's notebook. Look carefully at these ideas. Pick out any obvious, unoriginal ideas and find good new ideas of your own.

□ We hope you haven't lost those three ideas you thought of earlier! Produce a notebook page like the one about the walk through the wood. You do not have to write the poem at this stage.

Title?
Forest walk
Night creatures?
Midnight oaks?

TIME OF YEAR?
WEATHER?
WHY AM I THERE?
LOST? HUNTED?

Senses....

FEEL of tree trunks: rough, damp, smooth, Ivy?

SOUNDS: Foxes? distant traffic? owls hooting?
twigs cracking underfoot?
        Animals? Birds? Wind? Poacher's gun?
    SILENCE?

        Can I use metaphors and similes?
SCENTS? Smells of....

What about <u>movement</u>? How am I moving?
Running in panic? (Is the undergrowth wet/in
    a tangle/scratchy/impenetrable? Am I
    looking for something?)
Useful words:

Thicket	Creep	motionless
Copse	Scutter	bending
glade	tangle	stifling
clearing	shuffle	whipping
bole	trudge	pelting
oak	creak	
beech	swipe	
coppice		
scrub		
fern		
fungus		

2 Birth of a Cinquain

In this section, Judith Nicholls talks about how she wrote the poem *Celtic Burial Stones, 300 BC*. We then see a page from her notebook showing how the poem developed from the first jotted notes.

The whole class (9–11s) were on a five-day field trip at Wick Court, near Bristol. We had an excellent guide from the centre who was able to point out all manner of features we would otherwise have failed to notice – a badger's passageway through a hedge, a mediaeval pilgrim's way (just a lengthy dip in the ground to us) and so on.

The stones described in the cinquain stood alone, partly sunken, and apparently undistinguished in the middle of a field we walked through. Our guide pointed out the distant hill where the chieftain's last battle had been fought. I wanted to write something about them and made a few notes back at the field centre when the children wrote their evening 'diaries'.

In some ways the final version remains very similar to the initial one, but I feel that more meaning is concentrated into the final one. There are of course many limitations to what can be achieved with such a short form – a cinquain or haiku is perhaps less likely to 'sing' than many more extended forms can. However, from a writer's point of view I find it quite a good discipline to attempt from time to time – with so few words to play around with each one *has* to work for its place! (Hence the various 'word-searches' as the poem developed.)

'Lords' says more than 'stones' (and at the point when 'stones' was put in the title, it was no longer needed in the poem itself); 'shrouded' says more than 'mottled'; 'grey', 'shrouded', 'still' and 'silent' add to the feeling of death before the final word – and of course 'still' has more than one meaning, adding also the contrast of the long life of the stones and the short life of the chieftain . . . .

I tried several possible drafts the same evening and over the next two or three days before reaching the 'final' (?) one.

Lichen on a sinking stone...
Green lichen on a ~~rough~~ grey

Lichen wrapped against the centuries' weathers... winds?
lichen-laced

mottled? lichen-mottled grey stone

greystones
ages
mottled/chafed
feathers/mapped grey

1st Draft:

grey stones
mapped with lichen
sunk in an open field
cold reminders of a chieftain's
sad death

/proud or sad death?

Try some other ideas:

Lichen,
green on rough grey
~~softening~~
stones sinking in warm earth,
~~cold reminders~~ of a chieftain's
lost life/sad death

Landmark of lichen seas?
oceans, lichen mapped on...

grey stones   in
lichen-laced and
~~sunken-long~~
cold memorial to a chieftain's
proud death
          fall
memorial to a chieftain's last battle? Title...'Burial place of a
                                        Celtic chief, 333 BC'?

Try again:
'Burial Place, 300 B.C.'

Grey stones,
~~Laced with lichen~~
Stand proud in ~~open~~ a bare field,
~~proud~~ memorial to a chieftain's
Last fall

shaded
shrouded
screened
veiled
stooping
shadowed
bowed
bathed
fallen

Lichen –
Crusted grey stone
rests in secret earth, – silent?

mist
rest

Proud memorial to a chieftain's
sad death

still ?

Celtic Burial Stones, 300 BC

Lichen
Shrouded – stone grey
~~sentry~~ for guards of a silent earth
Still memorial As a chieftain's
sad death

lichen-shrouded
guards?

chill
once fell ?

laced
shaded
stooping
fallen
bathed
shadowed

guards of the hillside mist
guards ~~of~~ for a lonely hill
Still memorial ~~where a~~ to a chieftain's
~~once fell~~ last fall

Grey guards
Lords ~~knights~~ in a silent earth,   war- scarred earth ?

Grey lords,
lichen – shrouded
guards/guardians of a sad/silent earth;
Still memorial to a chieftain's
sad death.

full ?
dark ?

Celtic Burial Stones, 300 BC

Grey lords
lichen shrouded
guards of a silent earth;
still memorial to a chieftain's
sad death.

Notice that

— Judith Nicholls decided on the *form* of the poem early on and this
helped to shape the poem as it developed.

— She continually tried new words and ideas, but was prepared to go
back to her first ideas when she felt that they were the best after all.
The last line, for example, kept changing , but in the end she came
back to her first idea.

— Words tried out in one part of the poem came in useful somewhere
else. She didn't throw them away.

■ See how the word 'guards' finds its place in the poem.

This is how the last line of the poem developed:

> sad death
> proud death
> lost life
> last battle
> last fall
> sad death
> once fell
> sad death

■ Do you think Judith Nicholls has made the best choice? Can you think of an alternative ending? (Remember, it should only have two syllables.)

3 Instant Poems

In the last section we talked about starting a poem by scribbling down as many ideas as you can. Some poets prefer to start by having a go at the poem, not minding how bad it is to start with. Very often the first go is produced quickly – in just a minute or two.
    This method of starting is good because:

– it gives you something to hang your ideas on.
– it gives you an overall 'plan'.

You are going to write some 'instant' starter poems. Remember, these are not finished poems yet, but just quick *ideas* for poems.

☐ In the work in the last section you wrote down three ideas for a poem based on your own memories. You will need to use one of these now. You are allowed:

– three minutes' thinking time (no writing)
– three minutes' writing time (still thinking!)

■ Don't be embarrassed if your attempt seems bad! One or two volunteers can now put their instant poems on the board. Discuss how they could be improved, and what could be added or taken away. You might end up with a final version, or the original writer might include some of the suggested ideas in a poem that he or she writes.

4 Jack O'Legs

In this section Wes Magee describes how he wrote the poem *The Legend of Jack O'Legs*. Wes Magee prefers to start by having a first go at writing a poem.

My poem about Jack O'Legs 'happened' in Hertfordshire, in the village of Weston. Weston . . . a quiet place, tucked away in rich countryside to the north of Stevenage, a settlement complete with duck pond, village green and parish church.

It was to visit the church that I drove to Weston on a chilly November day in 1976.

I parked my car in a lane close to the church. A handful of rooks circled above tall trees. The square tower loomed large. A rusty gate led to a flag-stoned path through the churchyard. A weather-beaten headstone close to the path caught my attention. It was unmarked, and some four metres away stood a smaller footstone. The great length of the grave was a puzzle. He must have been a giant, I muttered to myself.

The church itself was moderately interesting. I purchased a 30p guide book, and left.

Back in the comparative warmth of the car I idly flicked through the booklet. It contained the usual lists of names and dates, the expected architectural notes. A title, on the last page, took my eye . . . *The Legend of Jack O'Legs*. I read the brief story, and re-read it with growing interest.

I learned that centuries ago – in Weston Wood – there dwelled an astonishingly tall man. He could peer through an *upstairs* window and made a meagre living robbing travellers. Yet he never harmed the villagers of Weston. They gave him the name Jack O'Legs.

During one particularly hard winter when food stocks in the village were getting low, Jack walked to nearby Baldock and stole sacks of grain from a mill. These he presented to the hungry villagers. During that snow-bound winter he paid many visits to the mill.

In desperation, the miller and his mates set a trap for Jack O'Legs. They caught him, beat him with sticks and put out his eyes. Jack O'Legs, knowing he was to die, pleaded to be granted one final request. He said, 'Let me fire one arrow and where it lands . . . there bury me.'

The miller agreed to this strange request. He handed Jack a bow. Jack's last arrow flew three miles, eventually striking the tower of Weston church. It fell to the churchyard, and there Jack O'Legs was buried.

A macabre story. I closed the guide book and retraced my steps into the churchyard. Once more I gazed at the headstone, at that incredibly long grave. Dusk was gathering. Winter was in the air.

Some months later I wrote a poem about the experience. I was attracted to the story of Jack O'Legs and wanted to capture on paper my feelings on that cold day in the churchyard. From the start I took *Legend* as my title. However, the first attempt (or draft) was not encouraging . . .

Legend (for Jack O'Legs)

So tall he conversed with the villagers
through their bedroom windows.
He was stronger than the beam of a barn.
A thief, he was ambushed, bound,
and had his eyes put out.
The men cut him about.
So ended his particular lesson.

Draft 1 failed to set the scene, or even properly retell the story. The last line seemed feeble, inadequate. What was I trying to say?

I tried again. Draft 2 seemed more substantial.

Legend (for Jack O'Legs)

Tall enough to converse with villagers
through their bedroom windows, and strong.
One snow-filled winter he stole from a mill,
carting off three sacks of flour at one lift.

Ambushed, he was bound and his eyes poked out.
Atrocities are easy once first blood is spilled.
Imagine, for a moment the pain in that lane.
But then, he was permitted to fire an arrow

and where it landed they buried him,
stone at his feet, stone at his head.
Measure him today, how tall he walked in his time.
Think how he was chopped down to size.

Um. The story seemed unclear. Jack's character failed to come alive. Even so, the 'poem' was taking shape. Three verses had emerged, each with four lines. The poem, though, did not flow; it did not read well. I worked hard and completed more drafts.

By Draft 10 the writing had tightened, the narrative was firmer. Each line was in the region of ten syllables long and I was using this idea as a method of building and controlling the writing. The length of sentences varied, but there was a terse, taut feeling which added to the horror of the legend. At last, I felt, the poem was communicating something of the scene, the cold winter, the man who had been Jack O'Legs.

Legend (for Jack O'Legs)

He was a freak, so tall he could look
through upstairs bedroom windows and talk with
the villagers as they lay in their beds.

Helpful, too. One hard, snow-marooned winter
he strode across buried fields and stole sacks
of flour from a distant mill. His friends ate.

That act signed his death-warrant. The miller
gathered toughs and ambushed him in a copse.
He was bound, savaged, and his eyes poked out.

A last request: he fired an arrow three miles
and asked to be buried where it landed.
Then they struggled to hang him from a tree.

The shape of the poem had improved, but many points were still wrong . . . .

Verse 1, line 3: '*the* villagers as *they* lay in *their* beds'. That was repetitive, dull.

Verse 2: Was 'hard' necessary in line 1? Surely 'snow-marooned' communicated the idea of a 'hard winter'. In line 3, 'His friends ate.' sounded blunt and awkward.

Verse 4: Lines 1 and 2 sounded too chatty, too easy for such a terrible situation.

Verse 4: The final word 'tree' was not the right word. But what word was needed?

During the next few days the poem progressed. I was now at the polishing stage. For a time I left the poem alone in order to come back to it fresh, in order to gain a sense of distance.

The poem completed itself at around Draft 20. It had grown to five verses, and each line contained nine syllables. Such a mathematical construction seemed to suit the story; it helped to keep the legend direct. There was little room for padding. I now felt that I had managed to recreate a time long ago, a time of harsh winters and wayside brutality. Quite deliberately I avoided making my own comment in the poem. I wanted the reader to understand for himself/herself the sense of tragedy and strangeness. Had I, though, managed to convey that bond I had felt with Jack O'Legs as I stood beside his long grave? Only the reader of the poem can answer that question . . . .

Legend (for Jack O'Legs)

He was a freak, so tall he could gawk
Through upstairs bedroom windows and talk
With villagers as they lay in bed.

Helpful, too. One snow-marooned winter
He strode buried fields, stole sacks of flour
From a distant mill and fed his friends.

That act was decisive; the miller
Gathered toughs, ambushed him in a copse.
He was bound, knifed, and his eyes gouged out.

Before the end they granted one wish,
Handed him a bow from which he loosed
A shaft. Where it fell – three miles away –

They agreed to dig his grave. And so
To the main business of that cold day.
Six men strove to hang him from an oak.

Final notes: 'gawk' means 'to stare stupidly'.
   I eventually chose the word 'oak' to end the poem. It seemed a sturdy tree from which to hang a very tall man, and said aloud has a clipped, snap ending . . . rather like the sound of a neck breaking!

5 Drafting

Wes Magee had twenty goes before *Legend* 'completed itself'.
Rewriting or drafting is important. We are trying to shape our original
idea into the poem we want.

When you are drafting you will need to think about:

> The *shape* or *form* of the poem.
> – regular rhythm or not?
> – long poem or short poem?
> – long lines or short lines?
> – will there be rhyme?
>
> The *language* of the poem
> – choosing words
> – metaphors and similes

When you have finished the first attempt, you will need to:

> Read it out loud to yourself.
> Read it to others (your teacher, other pupils)

Underline the bits that are not right. Have another go.
There are several dangers.

Repeating yourself

Examples: 'The foggy day was grey with mist . . .'; 'The white snow lay
covering the ground'.
(What colour is snow likely to be? Do you need 'lay' and 'covering'?)

Unoriginal ideas

Examples: 'The cat was as black as soot . . .'; 'I walked through the
wood at night. Owls hooted, and twigs cracked underfoot . . .'.

Ideas that are nothing to do with the subject

You often come up with interesting words and phrases when you are
writing a poem. The trouble is, they may not really 'fit'. You may be so
pleased with the ideas that you want to keep them in. This is a mistake.
Remember, you can always save up the ideas and use them in another
piece of writing.

Rotten rhymes

Poems do not have to rhyme, but if you decide that your poem will,
the rhymes should be natural, not put in just for the rhyme. It is
tempting sometimes to stick in a silly rhyme because you can't think of
a better one. Don't! Remember, there is more than one type of rhyme.

Epitaph

Beneath these high Cathedral stairs
Lie the remains of Susan Pares.
Her name was Wiggs, it was not Pares,
But Pares was put to rhyme with stairs.

EDWARD LEAR

☐ Read Wes Magee's Poem *Electric Household* on page 81. Write a
  list poem of your own.

Not all the things that Wes Magee mentions are appliances – electric
shocks are included! There are many possible topics for a 'list' poem,
such as zoos, pop stars, TV programmes, jobs, and untidy bedrooms!

☐ Volunteers only! We wrote 'instant poem starters' and put some of
  them on the board. This time, put a finished poem on the board. See
  how many 'dangers' you can find.

6 And Finally . . .

The shortest section of the book! This section puts a very difficult
question:

> *How do you know when the poem is finished?*

Possible answers are:
– when you are satisfied with it
– when you think you can't do any more to it
– when you are tired of it! (you can always come back to it later)

There is no point rewriting just for the sake of it; it is possible to lose
good ideas as well as to improve your poem. Sometimes, if you are
very lucky, a poem can 'arrive' with almost no drafting at all.

North York Moors: November

A first raw wind of winter
Is shaving the moors' gaunt face:
Rain stings the heather, rocks smart,
Sheep are like flecks of lather.

From the steamed car's safety
You view a dark land; slant sky
Greying with worry and fret.
Ridges, tops trawl rags of cloud.

The bleak landscape is littered
With outcrops; stone defining
The region's tongue, its guttural
And blunt consonantal clash.

How your car shivers in the
Wind's strop, the astringent air.
Ahead, a thin-clad road clings
To skinned and heaving contours.

Breakdown

Old bull nose truck,
   a nerve-exposed hulk,
ganglions ragged and torn.
   No escape from
the rash of nettles
   or rain's slow erosion.
A rusting wreck
   sunk deep in seabed weeds,
it is cannibalised
   by spare-part hunters.
Like a harassed mother
   beset by clamorous children
it buckles, goes under,
   nerve-ends on display,
its life slowly breaking down.

iron light bulb
  tv dryer
cooker blanket
  toothbrush fire
'fridge radio
  shaver clock
toaster speaker
  auto lock
pump hair crimper
  robot drill
vacuum cleaner
  kettle grill
slicer grinder
  meters fan
wires tea maker
  deep fry pan
slide projector
  fuses shocks
freezer bulkhead
  junction box
water heater
  time switch lamps
knife recorder
  cables amps
torch computer
  mixer plug

telephone switch
  socket bug
door chimes organ
  infra red
guitar video
  sunlamp bed
heated rollers
  current watts
train adaptor
  washer spots
synthesiser
  magic door
trimmer dimmer
  power saw
headphones curler
  night light glow
calculator
  stereo
bell typewriter
  camera flash
watches mowers
  mince-a-trash
cultivator
  metronome
volts vibrator
  ohm sweet ohm

Visitor

Sliding in slippers along the house-side
you find the fragments of the turkey's carcase
beside the toppled dustbin lid, and there
on the lawn's snow quilt a line of paw marks.

Town fox, that wraith of winter, soundlessly
thieved here as frost bit hard and stars shivered.
This bleak morning, under a raw-boned sky,
you stoop to examine the frozen tracks

and print yours where a spectral guest came late
to share a Christmas dinner. Around the
gable-end a starved wind razors and from
the split gutters icicles hang like fangs.

Cries of London

the busker and his echoes in the subway
   the fans wild-singing on the train
  the mugged girl weeping in the precinct
    the rain

the marchers and their banner-calls for justice
   the juke-box belting through the bars
  the old jane cursing in the washroom
    the cars

the billboards with their claims and scarlet language
   the crazed drunk yelling out his fears
  the news-stands brash and bold with headlines
    the tears

the dancers as they fall out from the disco
   the weirdo beat up by the boys
  the wet streets filled with feet and voices
    the noise

A Marked Man

December.
A boy named
'Grooly' Pugh
skates over
the wintry
school tarmac.
'Sir, for you,'

and hands me
a paper ball,
a damp clot
then slopes off,
slithering.
Hail and sleet
like grapeshot.

Numb fingered
I unfold
a moist sheet
and there see
(shivering,
my bones cold)
the black spot.